Y0-BZG-032

Families In Their Neighborhoods

EVERYDAY LEARNING™

CHICAGO, ILLINOIS

Everyday Learning Development Staff

Editorial: Amber Krieger, Steve Mico, Leslie Morrison
Production/Design: Fran Brown, Dan Lampert, Eric Olson

Illustrations

Inside cover, Herman Adler Design Group; Table of Contents (bottom) Kathi Ember;
4-5 Kathi Ember; 6-7 Herman Adler Design Group; 8-9 Kathi Ember; 10-11 Kathi Ember;
12-13 Donna Nelson; 18-19 Kathi Ember; 20-21 Mapping Specialists.

Photo Credits

Cover (background photo), © A. Gurmankin/Unicorn Stock Photos; Cover (left), © Robert E. Daemmrich/
Tony Stone Images; Cover (right), © Lawrence Manning/Tony Stone Images; Cover (bottom),
© Tom McCarthy/Unicorn Stock Photos; 3 (left), © Photri; 3 (top right and bottom right), © SuperStock
International, Inc.; 4 (left), © A. Gurmankin/Unicorn Stock Photos; 4 (right), © Tony Freeman/PhotoEdit;
5 (top), © David Young-Wolff/PhotoEdit; 5 (bottom), © SuperStock International, Inc.; 6 (top),
© Bruce Forster/Tony Stone Images; 6 (bottom), © Jean Higgins/Unicorn Stock Photos; 7 (left),
© J.R. Page/Valan; 7 (center), © Aneal Vohra/Unicorn Stock Photos; 7 (right), © Jean Higgins/Unicorn
Stock Photos; 8 (left), © Robert E. Daemmrich/Tony Stone Images; 8 (top right), © Michael Newman/
PhotoEdit; 8 (bottom right), © Joel Dexter/Unicorn Stock Photos; 9 (top left), © Mary Kate Denny/
PhotoEdit; 9 (top right), © Betts Anderson/Unicorn Stock Photos; 9 (center), © SuperStock International,
Inc.; 9 (bottom), © Florent Flipper/Unicorn Stock Photos; 10 (top left), © SuperStock International, Inc.;
10 (bottom left), © Robert Brenner/PhotoEdit; 10 (bottom), © Tom McCarthy/PhotoEdit; 11 (top left),
© Cathlyn Melloan/Tony Stone Images; 11 (top right), © Tony Freeman/PhotoEdit; 11 (bottom),
© Robert Brenner/PhotoEdit; 14-15, © M. Bruce/Photri; 14 (top left), © Aneal Vohra/Unicorn Stock Photos;
14 (bottom left), © David Young-Wolff/PhotoEdit; 14 (bottom right), © Jeff Greenberg/Unicorn Stock
Photos; 15 (top), © Robert E. Daemmrich/Tony Stone Images; 15 (bottom left), © Michael Newman/
PhotoEdit; 15 (bottom right), © Photri; 16 (top left), © Tony Freeman/PhotoEdit; 16 (top right),
© David Young-Wolff/PhotoEdit; 16 (bottom), © Tom McCarthy/Unicorn Stock Photos; 17 (top),
© David Young-Wolff/PhotoEdit; 17 (bottom), © David Young-Wolff/PhotoEdit; 18 (left), © Y. R. Tymstra/
Valan; 18 (right) and 19 (top left), © Wolfgang Kaehler; 19 (top right), © Val & Alan Wilkinson/Valan;
19 (bottom left), © SuperStock International, Inc.; 19 (bottom right), © Wolfgang Kaehler; 22 (top),
© Lawrence Manning/Tony Stone Images; 22 (bottom), © Brian Seed/Tony Stone Images; 23 (background),
© Phil Schermeister/Tony Stone Images; 23 (top left), © Connie Geocaris/Tony Stone Images; 23 (top
right), © Jim Pickerell/Tony Stone Images; 23 (bottom left), © Photri; 23 (bottom right), © Gary Conner/
PhotoEdit; 24 (top left), © Aneal Vohra/Unicorn Stock Photos; 24 (top center), © A. Gurmankin/Unicorn
Stock Photos; 24 (top right), © Robert E. Daemmrich/Tony Stone Images; 24 (center left), © David Young-Wolff/
PhotoEdit; 24 (center center), © SuperStock International, Inc.; 24 (center right), © M. Bruce/Photri;
24 (bottom left), © Aneal Vohra/Unicorn Stock Photos; 24 (bottom center), © Wolfgang Kaehler;
24 (bottom right), © Jeff Greenberg/Unicorn Stock Photos; 25 (top right), © Photri; 25 (center left),
© David Young-Wolff/PhotoEdit; 25 (center center), © Tony Freeman/PhotoEdit; 25 (bottom left),
© Tony Freeman/PhotoEdit; 25 (bottom center), © Michael Newman/PhotoEdit; 25 (bottom right),
© David Young-Wolff/PhotoEdit; 25 (bottom left), © Tony Freeman/PhotoEdit; 25 (bottom right),
© David Young-Wolff/PhotoEdit; Photo research by Feldman & Associates.

ISBN 1-57039-102-5

23456789 CP 0403020100

Contents

Neighborhoods

People live together in neighborhoods.
There are many different kinds of neighborhoods.

▲ In a city, many people live and work in a small area. Buildings and houses are usually close together. Tall apartment and office buildings hold a lot of people without using very much land.

▲ Suburbs are less crowded areas next to cities. Houses can be larger and not as close together. People who live in suburbs may have lawns and gardens.

People who move or travel a lot can live in trailer homes. A trailer home has wheels and can be pulled by a car. Trailer home neighborhoods are called trailer parks. ▶

▲ Farmers need a lot of land to grow their crops and raise their animals. So in a farm neighborhood, houses are often far apart.

Homes and Neighborhoods

Here is a trailer park. We can make a map of this neighborhood.

Types of Homes

Homes are made of different materials in different climates and regions. People want to use materials that last a long time, are easy to get, and will protect them from the weather.

▲ Adobe is clay that is dried in the sun. Adobe homes are perfect for hot, dry climates because they keep the heat outside and the cool air inside.

A Neighborhood Map

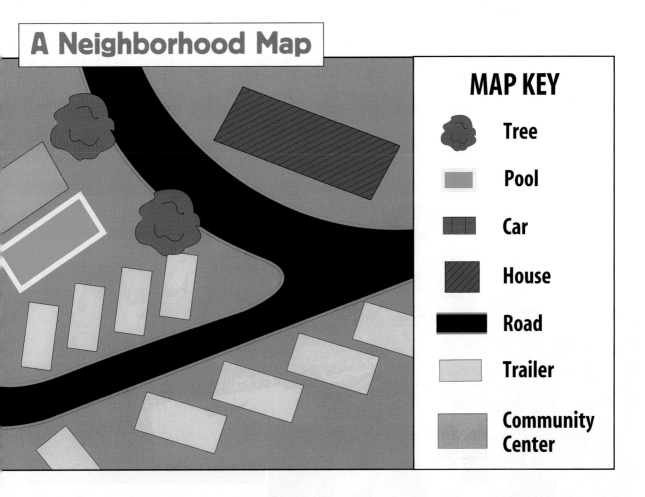

MAP KEY

- Tree
- Pool
- Car
- House
- Road
- Trailer
- Community Center

▲ People may live in a log cabin in a place where there are lots of trees.

Many older homes are made from bricks. Bricks are strong and last a long time. ▼

This beach house is built on stilts so that water will not get in the house. ▼

Families

Family members help each other when they have work to do.
Family members can learn from each other as they work.
And when families work together, they grow closer.

Families also grow closer when they play together.
Families have special ways to have fun together.
What do you do for fun with your family?

Families Are Neighbors

What do you like to do with your neighbors?

Neighbors work together to make the neighborhood a nice place to live.

▲ Neighbors help each other when they are in need.

▲ These people are holding a car wash to raise money for a sick neighbor.

▲ These neighbors are building a barn together.

Problems in the Neighborhood

Sometimes there are problems in the neighborhood.
Neighbors need to work together to solve the problems.
What problems do you see in this neighborhood?

Solving Problems

A neighborhood is part of a community. When people need information or help solving problems they can turn to other members of the community.

firefighters ▶

▲ garbage collectors

▲ librarian

▲ postal worker

Community Meetings

Neighbors can hold meetings to talk about ways to solve problems and improve the neighborhood. Neighbors can learn new ways to solve problems from each other. Neighbors listen to each other's ideas and agree on ways to keep the neighborhood clean and safe.

▲ teacher

police officer ▲

Making a Difference

One way neighbors can make a difference is to start a recycling program. Recycling means using things again instead of throwing them away. People can recycle plastic, glass, paper, and cans. Recycling centers use these materials to make new things.

When neighbors work together and follow the rules, the neighborhood becomes a clean, safe, and fun place to live!

Street Signs

Street signs can tell people what the rules are. Signs can make a neighborhood safer.

SLOW
CHILDREN

Pitch In!
Put trash
in its place

DANGER
NO
TRESPASSING

Around the World

People all over the world live in neighborhoods. Many people live in traditional homes, the same kinds of homes their families have lived in for years. These homes are usually made from local materials. Other people live in cities that look a lot like cities in the United States.

▲ Otavalo, Ecuador
Otavalo Indians use local materials to build their homes. The walls are made from mud, and the roof is straw.

▲ Thimphu, Bhutan
In cities all around the world, most people live in homes made from wood or bricks.

Timbuktu, Mali

The Tuareg tribe are nomads, which means they move around a lot. They live in tents that are easy to pack and move.

▼

▲ Western Norway

These homes are raised on piles of stone. How do you think this helps when it snows in winter?

▲ Corfe Village, England

These old homes are made from stone. Stone is very strong but costs more than brick, so people don't usually use it for homes anymore.

▲ Tonle Sap Lake, Cambodia

Every spring and summer this lake floods the land around it. People can live in homes on stilts or houseboats like these to stay dry.

A World Map

Where in the world are the neighborhoods you just read about?

NORTH AMERICA

Corfe Village, England

United States

Atlantic Ocean

Timbuktu, M-

Otavalo, Ecuador

SOUTH AMERICA

Pacific Ocean

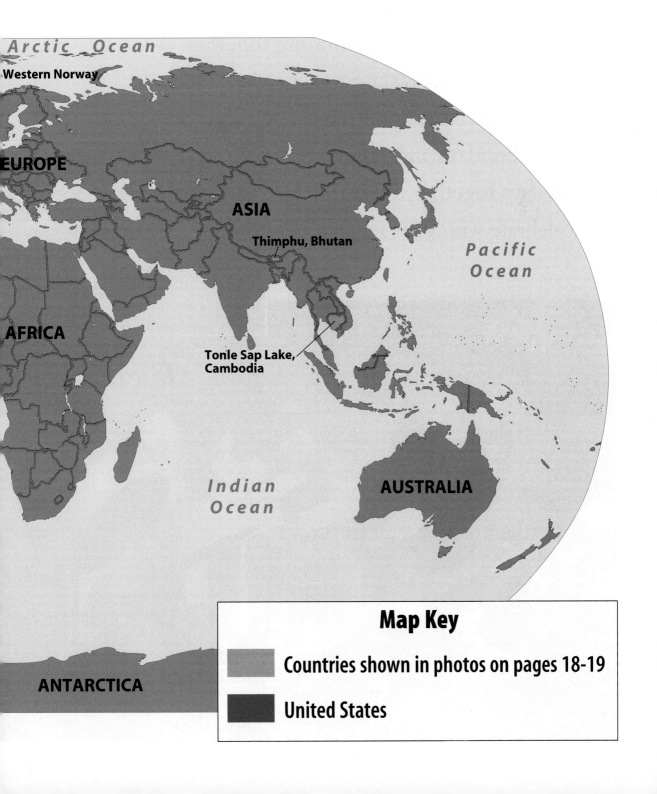

Arctic Ocean

Western Norway

EUROPE

ASIA

Thimphu, Bhutan

Pacific Ocean

AFRICA

Tonle Sap Lake, Cambodia

Indian Ocean

AUSTRALIA

ANTARCTICA

Map Key

Countries shown in photos on pages 18-19

United States

Celebrating with Neighbors

Neighbors celebrate together in many ways and for many reasons. Celebrating together helps neighbors get to know each other. Neighbors celebrate traditions as well as holidays and other special days together. How do you celebrate with your neighbors?

Glossary

apartment building
page 7

city
page 4

community meeting
page 15

crossing guard
page 17

farm
page 5

firefighters
pages 14-15

garbage collectors
page 14

houseboat
page 19

librarian
page 14